JUN 18

MORE

D0367248

FRENCH SLANGUAGE

A FUN VISUAL GUIDE TO FRENCH TERMS AND PHRASES BY MIKE ELLIS

GIBBS SMITH
TO ENRICH AND INSPIRE HUMANKIND

DEDICATED TO SUZANNE, VIRGINIA, MIKEY, AND PHIDGETTE

First Edition
22 21 20 19 18   5 4 3 2 1

Text © 2018 Mike Ellis
Illustrations © 2018 Rupert Bottenberg, except illustrations
of monkey on pages 8, 13, 60, 74, 79, 89 © 2018 yyang/
Shutterstock.com; ant on page 9 © 2018 designer_an/
Shutterstock.com; money on page 12 © 2018 Uncle Leo/
Shutterstock.com; swan on page 14 © 2018 Patimat
Alieva/Shutterstock.com; pan on page 18 © 2018 Artslord/
Shutterstock.com; ape on pages 21, 55, 67, 75 © 2018
yyang/Shutterstock.com; trumpet player on page 24 ©
2018 red rose/Shutterstock.com; peace sign on page 28
© 2018 Gl0ck/Shutterstock.com; bowl on page 32 © 2018
vectorisland/Shutterstock.com; wheel on page 33 © 2018
Artsiom Zavadski/Shutterstock.com; barber pole on page
40 © 2018 totallypic/Shutterstock.com; bat on pages 43, 85
© 2018 VectorShots/Shutterstock.com; blade on page 44 ©
2018 Vectorcarrot/Shutterstock.com; palm tree on pages
46, 82 © 2018 korsaralex/Shutterstock.com; crow on pages
48, 55 © 2018 In Art/Shutterstock.com; knot on page 50 ©
2018 Wiktoria Pawlak/Shutterstock.com; apple on pages
57, 59 © 2018 Ellika/Shutterstock.com; apple core on page
71 and vase on page 77 © 2018 Rvector/Shutterstock.com

All rights reserved. No part of this book may be
reproduced by any means whatsoever without
written permission from the publisher, except
brief portions quoted for purpose of review.

Published by
Gibbs Smith
P.O. Box 667
Layton, Utah 84041

1.800.835.4993 orders
www.gibbs-smith.com

Designed by michelvrana.com

Gibbs Smith books are printed on paper produced
from sustainable PEFC-certified forest/controlled
wood source. Learn more at www.pefc.org.
Printed and bound in Hong Kong

Library of Congress Cataloging-in-Publication Data

Names: Ellis, Mike, 1961- author.
Title: More French slanguage : a fun
visual guide to French terms and
phrases / Mike Ellis.
Description: First edition. | Layton, Utah : Gibbs Smith, 2017.
Identifiers: LCCN 2017032648 | ISBN 9781423648291 (pbk.)
Subjects: LCSH: French language--
Conversation and phrase books--English.
Classification: LCC PC2121 .E454
2017 | DDC 448.3/421--dc23
LC record available at https://lccn.loc.gov/2017032648

CONTENTS

HOW TO USE THIS BOOK

If you have always wanted to learn the basics of French, but traditional methods seemed overwhelming or intimidating, this is the book for you! Just follow the directions below and soon you'll be able to say dozens of words and phrases in French.

• Follow the illustrated prompts and practice saying the phrase quickly and smoothly.

• Emphasize the words or syllables highlighted in red.

• A strikethrough means you don't pronounce that letter or letters.

• Learn to string together words or phrases to create many more phrases.

• Draw your own pictures to help with memorization and pronunciation.

• How to sound more fluent:
  - French "r"s are pronounced with your uvula—almost like you're clearing your throat.
  - Smoosh your words together to achieve a more convincing manner of speech.

Note: This book may produce Americanized French.

For free sound bytes, visit slanguage.com.

Hi/Bye (informal) *Salut*	**Sally Lou**
Hey there *Coucou*	**Coo Coo**
'Morning *'jour*	**Frasier**
'Evening *'soir*	**Swat**

Hello (on phone)
Allô

Ah Low

What's up?
Quoi de neuf?

Quad Enough

Are you well?
Ça va?

Sock Vah?

Delighted to meet you
Enchanté

On Shawn Tail

This is my buddy
C'est mon pote

Say Monkey Putt

Kisses, sweetie
Bisous, chouchou

Bee Zoo Shoe Shoe

Not bad
Pas mal

Pa Molly

Are you alone?
T'es tout seul?

Tail Toot Sole?

Safe journey
Bonne route

Bun Root

I have to go
Je dois y aller

Should Wash Bee Ah Lay

Gotta run!
Je dois filer

Should Wash Fee Lay

See you soon
À bientôt

Ah Bee Ant Toe

See you later
À plus tard

Up Lou Tar

Good night
Bonne nuit

Bun We

Goodbye
Au revoir

Oaf Wash

Do you serve . . . ?
Servez-vous . . . ?

Survey Voo . . . ?

I'd like . . .
Je voudrais . . .

Shove Voo Drain . . .

Enjoy your meal
Bon appétit

Ball Nap Pay Tee

It's magnificent
C'est magnifique

Say Money Feek

Delicious
Délicieux

Dell Lease You

Compliments to
the chef
Compliments au chef

Come Plea Monkey

Oh Chef

Fritters
Beignets

Ben Yay

Puff pastry strips
Allumettes

Al Lou Met

Charcuterie
Charcuterie

Shark Coo Tree

Tapenade
Tapenade

Top Pen Nod

Salad Niçoise
Salade Niçoise

Sal Odd Knee Swans

Coquilles Saint-Jacques
Coquilles Saint-Jacques

Comb Key Sang Shock

Bite-size morsel
Petites bouchées

Pet Tee Boo Shay

Carrot quiche
Quiche aux carottes

Key Show Care Oat

Quiche Lorraine
Quiche Lorraine

Key Sh'Low Rain

Chicken with sausage
Poulet à la saucisse

Pool Lay Allah Sew Cease

Crab soufflé
Soufflé au crabe

Sue Flay Oak Crab

Soft-boiled egg
Œuf à la coque

Uff Allah Coke

Onion tart
Tarte à l'oignon

Piperade with ham
Piperade au jambon

Scampi
Langoustine

Tart Alone Yawn

Pea Pay Rod Oak

James Bond

Long Goose Teen

Goose liver pate
Pâté de foie gras

Pat Tail Duh Fog Rock

Meat pie
Tourtière

Tour Tee Air

Chicken Parisienne
Poulet Parisienne

Pool Lay Pair Ease Yen

Rabbit with apples
Lapin aux pommes

Lot Pan Oh Pump

Steak tartare
Steak tartare

Steak Tar Tar

Coq au vin
Coq au vin

Cocoa Van

Snail cassolette
Cassolette d'escargots

Cass Oak Let Days

Car Go

Smoked sausage
from Morteau
Saucisse de Morteau

Sew Ceased More

Toe

Steak Bordelaise
Steak Bordelaise

Steak Bored Lays

Ratatouille
Ratatouille

Rat Uh Twee

Dieppe-style fish stew
Marmite dieppoise

Mar Meat D'Yep Was

Ape Was Dead Bore

Époisses from
Burgundy (cheese)
Époisses de Bourgogne

Gone Yeah

Fermier (cheese)
Fermier

Fur Me Yay

Mâconnais (cheese)
Mâconnais

Ma Cone Neigh

Valençay (cheese)
Valençay

Val Lawn Say

Consommé
Consommé

Con Sum May

Vichyssoise
Vichyssoise

Vee She's Was

Onion soup
Soupe a l'oignon

Soup Alone Yawn

Minestrone
Minestrone

Me Nest Rhone

Pistou soup
Soupe au pistou

Soup Oh Pea Stew

Baguette
Baguette

Bag Get

Bread *Pain*	**Pang**
Corn bread *Pain de maïs*	**Panned Mays**
Spice bread *Pain d'épices*	**Pang Day Peace** 
Whole wheat bread *Pain complet*	**Pang Come Play**

Pita bread
Pain pita

Pang Pea Top

Small roll
Petit pain

Pet Tee Pang

Ficelle
Ficelle

Fee Sell

Pinot blanc (wine)
Pinot blanc

Pea Know Blonk

Sémillon (wine)
Sémillon

Say Me Yawn

Muscadet (wine)
Muscadet

Moose Cod Day

Moët & Chandon
(champagne)
Moët & Chandon

Moe Way Shawn

Dawn

Sweets
Douceurs

Due Sir

Apple pie
Tarte aux pommes

Tar Toe Pump

Chocolate cake
Gâteau au chocolat

Got Toe Oh Show

Coal Lot

Chocolate bread
Pain au chocolat

Pang Oak Show Coal Lot

Gingerbread
Pain d'épices

Pang Day Peace

Chocolate mousse
Mousse au chocolat

Moose Oak Show

Coal Lot

Pie
Tarte

Tart

Banana soup
Soupe à la banane

Soup Allah Bun Nun

Strawberries
Fraises

Phrase

Crème Brûlée
Crème Brûlée

Crem Brew Lay

To cook/To bake
Cuire

Queer

To heat
Chauffer

Show Fay

Sautéed
Sautées

Sew Tail

Steamed
À la vapeur

Allah Vuh Purr

In foil
En papillote

On Pa Pea Oat

Bowl
Bol

Bowl

Measuring cup
Tasse à mesurer

Tassel May Zoo Ray

Garnish bouquet
Bouquet garni

Boo Kay Gar Knee

Olive oil
Huile d'olive

Wheel Doll Leave

To cut
Couper

Coo Pay

Julienne
Julienne

Julie Yen

Chiffonade
Chiffonnade

She Phone Nod

Oven *Four*	**4**
Refrigerator *Réfrigérateur*	**Ref Free Shape Rot Turn**
Fridge *Frigo*	**Free Go**
Flour *Farine*	**Far Reen**

Dough
Pâte

Pot

Shaped dough
Pâton

Pot On

To knead
Pétrir

Pate Rear

Crumbs
Miettes

Me Yet

That's so beautiful
C'est si beau

Say See Bow

That's totally you
C'est tout à fait toi

Say 2 Tough Fate Wad

In style
À la mode

Allah Mode

It's out of style
C'est démodé

Say Day Moe Day

On sale
En solde

On Sold

It's a good deal
C'est une bonne affaire

Set Tune Bun Affair

Fashion show
Défilé de mode

Day Fee Laid Mode

High fashion
Haute couture

Oat Coo Tour

Salon
Salon

Sal Lawn

Hair bun
Chignon

Sheen Yawn

Jumpsuit
Combinaison

Comb Bee Neigh Sock

Trousers
Pantalon

Pawn Tail Lawn

Culottes
Culottes

Cool Oat

Sock Doll

Sandals
Sandales

Pleat
Pli

Plea

Hay Pole Let

Epaulette
Épaulette

Minaudière *Minaudière*	**Me Know Dee Air**
Earrings *Boudes d'oreilles*	**Boo Club Door Ray**
Tulle (fabric) *Tulle*	**Tool**
Cherry (color) *Cerise*	**Sarah Ease**

Classical music
Musique classique

Muse Eek Class Seek

Symphony
Symphonie

Sam Phone Knee

Drums
Batterie

Bat Tree

Edith Piaf
Édith Piaf

Aid It Pea Aft

Virtuoso *Virtuose*	**Veer 2 Owes**
Pop music *Musique pop*	**Muse Eek Pop**
Rap music *Musique rap*	**Muse Eek Hop**
Dubbed *Doublée*	**Due Blade**

Debate
Débat

Day Ball

Cartoon
Dessin animé

Days Ann Annie Maid

Comedies
Comédies

Comb May Dee

Theatrical stage setting
Mise-en-scène

Me Sock Send

Cannes Film Festival
Festival de Cannes

Face Tee Val'd Con

Golden Palm (award)
Palme d'Or

Palm Door

TV show
Émission télévisée

Aim Meese Yawn Tell

Lay Vee Say

TV remote controller
Zappeur

Zap Purr

VCR
Magnétoscope

Man Yet Toe Scope

Cutting-edge
Avant-garde

Have On Guard

Artistic optical illusion
Trompe-l'œil

Trump Lie

Sketches
Croquis

Crow Key

Paul Cézanne
Paul Cézanne

Paul Says Ann

Claude Monet
Claude Monet

Clod Moe Neigh

The *Mona Lisa*
(painting)
La Joconde

Lock Show Cone'd

| Text message | |
| Texto | **Text Toe** |

| Computer | |
| Ordinateur | **Or Deed Knot Turn** |

| E-mail | |
| Courriel | **Curry Yell** |

| Emoticon | |
| Frimousse | **Free Moose** |

Keyword
Mot-clé

Moe Clay

Newsfeed
Fil d'actualité

Feel Dock 2 Ollie Tail

Password
Mot de passe

Mode Pass

Software
Logiciel

Low-G See Yell

Status *Statut*	**Stat 2**
To access *Accéder*	**Ax Say Day** 
To click *Cliquer*	**Clean Kay**
To scroll *Faire défiler*	**Fair Day Fee Lay**

To type
Taper

Top Pay

USB drive
Clé USB

Clay You Ess Bee

Wi-Fi
Wifi

We Fee

Wireless
Sans fil

Song Feel

Battery
Pile

Peel

Electrode
Électrode

Elect Road

Experiment
Expérience

Ex Perry Yawns

Eyepiece
Oculaire

Oak Cue Lair

Microscope
Microscope

Me Crow Scope

Pestle
Pilon

Pea Lawn

Pipette
Pipette

Pea Pet

Test tube
Éprouvette

Ape Prove Vet

To accept
Accepter

To applaud
Applaudir

To appoint
Nommer

To ask
Demander

Accept Tail

Apple Low Deer

No May

Dim On Day

To attempt
Tenter

Taunt Tail

To begin
Commencer

Come On Say

To belong
Appartenir

Apart Ten Near

To boast
Se vanter

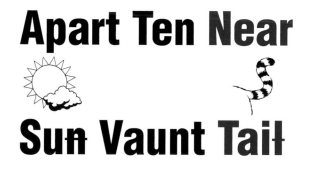
Sun Vaunt Tail

To call
Appeler

Apple Lay

To cancel
Annuler

Ann New Lay

To carry
Porter

Pour Tail

To cause
Causer

Comb Say

To clean
Nettoyer

To climb
Montée

To come
Venir

To congratulate
Féliciter

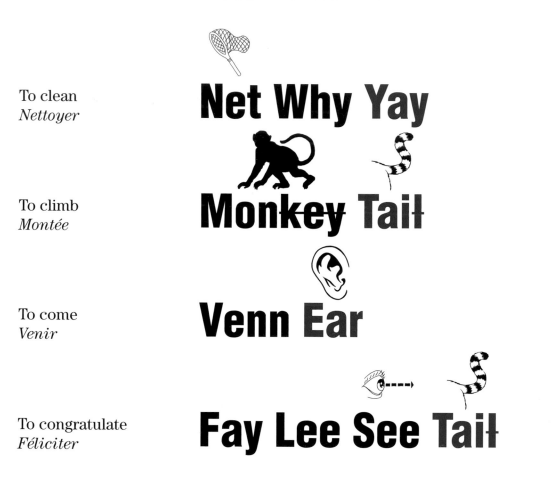

Net Why Yay

Monkey Tail

Venn Ear

Fay Lee See Tail

To continue
Continuer

Con Tee New Way

To cry
Pleurer

Plume Ray

To dare
Oser

Owe Say

To draw
Dessiner

Day See Neigh

To end
Terminer

Tare Me Neigh

To exist
Exister

Egg See Stay

To exit
Sortir

Sore Tier

To finish
Finir

Fee Near

To forgive
Pardonner

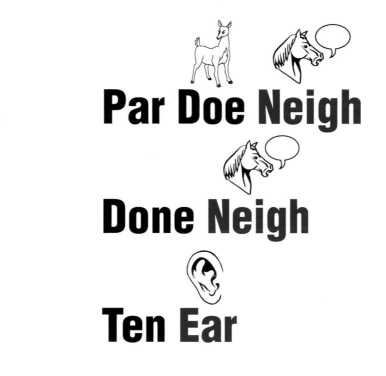

Par Doe Neigh

To give
Donner

Done Neigh

To hold
Tenir

Ten Ear

To hurt
Faire du mal

Fair Due Molly

To joke
Blaguer

Blog Gay

Men Neigh

To lead
Mener

To leave
Partir

Par Tier

To obtain
Obtenir

Hope Ten Ear

To occupy
Occuper

To pass
Passer

To put down
Poser

To quit
Quitter

Owe Cue Pay

Pa Say

Poe Say

Key Tail

To rent
Louer

Lou Way

To risk
Risquer

Risk Aim

To serve
Servir

Sarah Veer

To sniff
Renifler

Run Knee Flay

To speak
Parler

Par Lay

To spell
Épeler

Ape Lay

To squeeze
Presser

Pray Say

To suggest
Proposer

Pro Pose Say

To support	**Sue Ten Ear**
Soutenir	

To suppose	**Sue Pose Say**
Supposer	

To take away	**Ump Or Tail**
Emporter	

To take notes	**No Tail**
Noter	

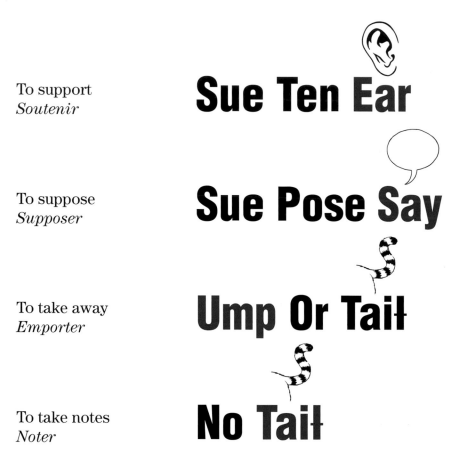

To touch
Toucher

2 Shay

To whine
Pleurnicher

Plural Knee Shay

To work
Bosser

Bow Say

To worry
Inquiéter

On Key Yet Tail

Above all
Surtout

Sir 2

Again
Encore

On Core

Already
Déjà

Day Shop

Angry
En colère

Uncle Air

Bald
Chauve

Show've

Blurry
Flou

Flu

Broken
Cassé

Cass Say

Busy
Occupé

Owe Cue Pay

Poe Tell Lay

Chubby
Potelé

Claire

Clear
Clair

Boo Clay

Curly
Bouclé

Share

Dear
Cher

Dry
Sec

Sect

Enormously
Énormément

Eh Nor May Monkey

Enough
Assez

Us Say

Everywhere
Partout

Par 2

Excited
Excité

Ex See Tay

Exhausted
Epuisé

Ape Wheeze Aim

False
Faux

Phone

Fashionable
À la mode

Allah Mode

First
D'abord

Dad Bore

Flexible
Souple

Sue Plus

Full of . . .
Plein de . . .

Planned . . .

Gifted
Doué

Due Way

Heavy
Lourd

Lured

Am Poe Lee

Impolite
Impoli

Impulsive
Impulsif

Am Pool See'f

Irritated
Enervé

Ann Nerve Vase

Large
Gros

Grow

Late
Tard

Tar

Nowhere
Nulle part

New'll Par

Outside
Dehors

Day Or

Plump
Grassouillet

Politely
Poliment

Precisely
Précisément

Proud
Fier

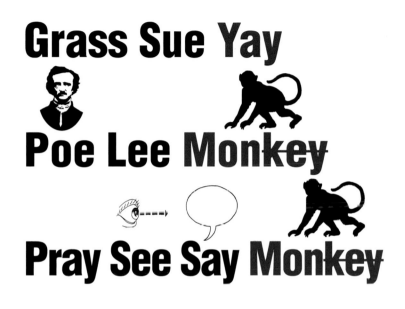

Grass Sue Yay

Poe Lee Monkey

Pray See Say Monkey

Fee Air

Public
Public

Poo Bleak

Short-sighted
Myope

Me Open

Smooth
Lisse

Lease

So/Then
Alors

Ap Lore

Such
Tel

Tell

Suddenly
Soudain

Sudan

Sweet
Doux

Due

There
La

Lock

Therefore *Donc*	**Donkey**

Thus *Ainsi*	**A~~nn~~ See**

Tiny *Minuscule*	**Me New School**

Tipsy *Pompette*	**Palm Pet**

Very *Très*	**Tray**
Wavy *Ondulé*	**On Due Lay**
Worn out *Fatigué*	**Fatty Gay**
Yesterday *Hier*	**He Air**

To the café *Au café*	**Oh Calf Fay**
To the park *Au parc*	**Oh Park**
To the coast *Sur la côte*	**Sir La Coat**
To go boating *Aller faire du bateau*	**Al Lay Fair Due Bat Toe**

To the hospital
A l'hôpital

Ah Low Pea Tall

Elementary school
École primaire

Aim Cole Pre Mare

Police department
Service de police

Serve Eased Poe

Lease

Post office
La poste

Lo~~c~~k Post

Subway
Métro

Mate Row

Arc de Triomphe
Arc de Triomphe

Ark'd Tree Umph

Bastille
Bastille

Bus Teal

Cannes
Cannes

Con

Carcassonne
Carcassonne

Carcass Sewn

Chamonix
Chamonix

Shah Moe Knee

Dome of the Invalids
Dôme des Invalides

Dome Days Ann Val Leed

Eiffel Tower
Tour Eiffel

Tour Ray Fell

Orsay Museum
Musée d'Orsay

Muse Say Door Say

Marseille
Marseille

Mar Say

Mont Saint Michel
Mont Saint-Michel

Monkey Sammy Shell

Nice
Nice

Niece

Sorbonne
Sorbonne

Sore Bun

Toulouse
Toulouse

2 Lose

Versailles
Versailles

Very Sigh

Dude
Mec

Nice
Sympa

Everything's cool
Ça roule

As usual
Comme d'hab

Make

Sam Pa

So~~ck~~ Rule

Come Dab

Fine (informal)
Ben

Ben

So-so
Comme ci, comme ça

Come See Come Sock

It's all good
Ça baigne

Sock Ben

Kid
Gamin

Gamble On

It's freezing
Ça caille

Sock Kite

Gross
Dégueulasse

Day Goose Lass

To freak out
Flipper

Flea Pay

Loser
Bolos

Bow Low

That's bizarre
C'est bizarre

Fishy
Chelou

Thanks a lot!
(sarcastic)
Cimer

Let's go
C'est parti

Say Bees Are

Shell Lou

See Mare

Say Par Tee

FRANGLISH

All these words (and more) are identical in spelling and meaning in English and French. Although you may experience small slanguage pronunciation differences, you will still be understood.

- Air
- Anaconda
- Appliqué
- Bandeau
- Bouquet
- Boutique
- Brunette
- Bustier
- Café

- Camouflage
- Cassette
- Chef
- Cliché
- Contact
- Correct
- Cuisine
- Direct
- Dragon

- E-mail
- Extra
- Golf
- Insect
- iPhone
- Mousse
- Okay
- Omelette
- Phish

- Piano
- Police
- Respect
- Rose
- Sofa
- Tube
- Volleyball
- Zoo